Grade
5

Unit
5

L·I·F·E·P·A·C®
History & Geography

ha Omega Publications ®

HISTORY & GEOGRAPHY 505
A NATION DIVIDED

W9-CBY-099

CONTENTS

Author: **Theresa Buskey, J.D.**
Editor: Alan Christopherson, M.S.
Illustrations: Brian Ring

Alpha Omega Publications ®

300 North McKemy Avenue, Chandler, Arizona 85226-2618
© MM by Alpha Omega Publications, Inc.   All rights reserved.
LIFEPAC is a registered trademark of Alpha Omega Publications, Inc.

A NATION DIVIDED

Seven states seceded from the Union after Abraham Lincoln was elected president in 1860. Shortly after that, the Union and the new Confederacy went to war. Four more states joined the Confederacy after the fighting began. The first section of this LIFEPAC® will cover the bloody, four year long Civil War which finally ended slavery in America.

After the war, the fighting continued during the time known as Reconstruction, which is covered in the second section. The South, which lost the war, was occupied by Union troops and forced to accept many changes in their laws and way of life. However, the South resisted, refusing to accept blacks as equals in law or life. Eventually, the North quit trying and the South succeeded in making blacks live separate lives with few rights or opportunities for almost one-hundred years.

The last section of this LIFEPAC is about the time after the Civil War. It was known as the Gilded Age. It was a time when many clever men became rich building new industries in America. It was also a time of widespread cheating in government and industry. The rich people put on an elegant show, but the nation was still divided, now between the rich and poor instead of the North and South.

OBJECTIVES

Read these objectives. The objectives tell you what you should be able to do when you have successfully completed this LIFEPAC.

When you have finished this LIFEPAC, you should be able to:

1. Describe the course of the Civil War and name the key battles.
2. Describe the strategies and advantages of each side.
3. Describe the course of Reconstruction and its major events.
4. Name the contents of the Thirteenth, Fourteenth and Fifteenth Amendments to the Constitution.
5. Describe life in the Gilded Age in America.
6. Explain how the railroad and Homestead Act encouraged settlement of the Great Plains.
7. Name some of the key people of the era and their accomplishments.
8. Describe some of the problems of the Gilded Age and the attempts to correct them.

VOCABULARY

Study these new words. Learning the meanings of these words is a good study habit and will improve your understanding of this LIFEPAC.

blockade (blo kād'). The blocking of a place by an army or navy to control who or what goes into or out of it

bond (bond). A certificate issued by a government which promises to pay back with interest the money borrowed from the buyer of the certificate

comedy (kom' ə dē). An amusing play or show having a happy ending

contract (kon' trakt). An agreement, often in writing, by which two or more people promise to do certain things; it can be enforced by law.

corporation (kôr' pə rā' shən). A group of persons who obtain a charter giving them, as a group, certain rights and privileges; a corporation can buy and sell, own property, manufacture and ship products as if it was a real person.

corrupt (kə rupt'). Influenced by bribes; dishonest

dominate (dom' ə nāt). To control or rule by strength or force

emancipate (i man' sə pāt). To set free from slavery of any kind

epidemic (ep' ə dem' ik). The rapid spreading of a disease so that many people have it at the same time

homespun (hōm' spun). Cloth made of yarn spun at home

infection (in fek' shən). A causing of disease in people by bringing them into contact with germs

junction (jungk' shən). A place of joining or meeting

lavish (lav' ish). To give or spend very freely or too freely

moral (môr' əl). Virtuous according to civilized standards or right and wrong; just

pension (pen' shən). A regular payment by an employer to a person who is retired or disabled

ruthless (rüth' lis). Having no pity; showing no mercy

scandal (skan' dl). A shameful action that brings disgrace or shocks public opinion

slum (slum). A run-down, overcrowded part of a city or town

tactless (takt les). Lack of skill in dealing with people or handling difficult situations

timid (tim' id). Easily frightened

Note: These words appear in **boldface** print the first time they are used in this LIFEPAC. If you are unsure of the meaning when you are reading, review the definition.

Pronunciation Key: hat, āge, cãre, fär; let, ēqual, tėrm; it, īce; hot, ōpen, ôrder; oil; out; cup, pút, rüle; child; long; thin; /ŦH/ for then; /zh/ for measure; /ə/ represents /a/ in about, /e/ in taken, /i/ in pencil /o/ in lemon, and /u/ in circus.

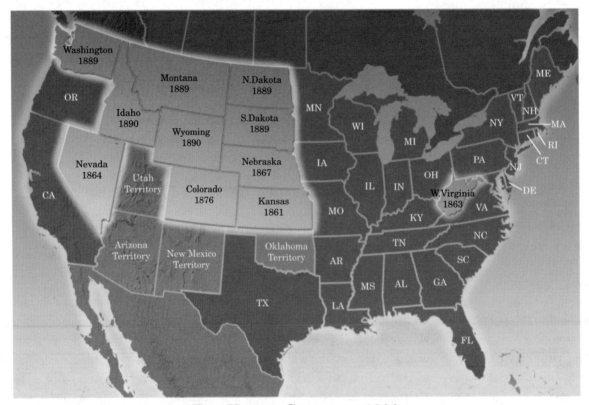

THE UNITED STATES IN 1890

2

I. THE CIVIL WAR

The Civil War lasted from 1861 to 1865. It was a bitter, bloody war. More Americans died in the Civil War than in any other war except World War II! Many families had men fighting on opposite sides. New rifles that could fire rapidly left thousands of men dead or wounded in just a one-day battle. The war was fought with all the bitterness and hatred of a divided family.

The Civil War began as a war to restore the Union and became a war against slavery. The Union (the North) had many problems trying to find the right general to lead their army. The Confederacy (the South) won many important battles, but in the end, the huge resources of the North wore them down. The Union eventually won by blockading the Confederate coast, taking control of the Mississippi River, and destroying the armies of the South.

Review these objectives. When you have completed this section, you should be able to:

1. Describe the course of the Civil War and name the key battles.
2. Describe the strategies and advantages of each side.

Restudy these words.

blockade	emancipate	homespun
infection	junction	moral
timid		

Starting and Strategy

War Comes. Abraham Lincoln was elected president in November of 1860. He was not inaugurated as president until March of 1861 (that was the law at the time). During that time, seven states led by South Carolina seceded and formed the Confederate States of America or the Confederacy with Jefferson Davis as president. The Confederacy had a constitution similar to the United States except it protected slavery and forbade tariffs. Its first capital was Montgomery, Alabama.

The U.S. president, James Buchanan, did nothing to stop the split. Several people did try to find a compromise that would stop the division of the country. The most important attempt was the *Crittenden Compromise*, proposed by Senator John Crittenden of Kentucky (a border state). It would have protected slavery south of the Missouri Compromise line by federal law, but both sides rejected the idea.

Lincoln acted calmly after he finally became president in March. He did not believe the southern states could leave the Union simply because they did not like the election results. However, he did not want to

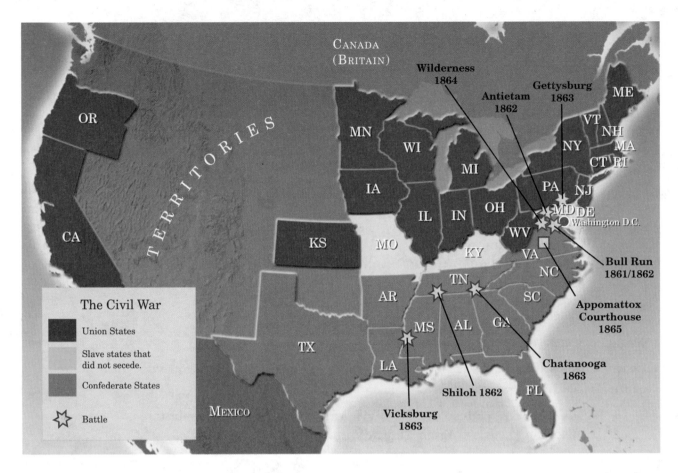

The Civil War

Union States

Slave states that did not secede.

Confederate States

☆ Battle

CANADA (BRITAIN)

Wilderness 1864

Antietam 1862

Gettysburg 1863

ME

OR

MN

WI

MI

NY

VT

NH

MA

CT RI

PA

NJ

IA

IL

IN

OH

MD DE

Washington D.C.

CA

KS

MO

KY

WV

VA

Bull Run 1861/1862

TERRITORIES

AR

TN

NC

SC

Appomattox Courthouse 1865

MS

AL

GA

Chatanooga 1863

TX

LA

FL

Shiloh 1862

MEXICO

Vicksburg 1863

start a war. Matters were taken out of his hands on April 12, 1861 when Confederate troops in South Carolina opened fire on Fort Sumter, a Union fort in Charleston harbor. Lincoln immediately called for volunteers to fill the Union army. The men of the North responded in huge numbers, furious that the "rebels" had fired on the American flag. This was the beginning of the Civil War.

The start of the war convinced several more southern states to leave the Union. Virginia, Arkansas, Tennessee, and North Carolina seceded after Fort Sumter, bringing the total number of Confederate states to eleven. The Confederate capital was then moved to Richmond, Virginia, just 120 miles from Washington, D.C. However, the counties in northwest Virginia refused to secede and later joined the Union as the state of West Virginia. Four slave states along the border (Missouri, Kentucky, Maryland, and Delaware) also stayed with the Union.

Strengths and Weaknesses. The Union had far more resources than the South in

this war. It had more men, factories, railroads, farms, and ships. That meant the Union had a bigger army, could equip it with more guns and ammunition, could move it to battle faster, and could feed and supply it better than the Confederacy. The Union could also use its navy to stop southern trade while Union ships continued to trade with Europe for guns and supplies.

The Confederates did not think those advantages were important. They were very proud of themselves and their "superior way of life." They did not believe that Yankee (northern) shopkeepers and factory workers could fight as well as southern gentlemen. The South also had some of its own advantages.

The Confederate army had much better generals than the Union and the Confederate soldiers were fighting for their way of life on their own land. The North had to defeat the South, capture their armies, and occupy their land to win. The South had only to survive to win.

The Confederacy also hoped to get help from Europe as America had in the Revolutionary War. Much of the cotton used to make cloth in British factories came from the southern United States in the 1860s. The Confederacy expected Britain to come to their aid to keep British cotton mills working. However, the Union sold Britain wheat and corn to feed its people. Also, many people in Britain hated slavery, so Britain stayed out of the war.

Northern Strategy. The Union had a basic strategy, or plan that it followed throughout the Civil War. The first part of the Union strategy was to use a navy **blockade** of the ports in the south. This kept the South from getting supplies it desperately needed. At first, blockade runners (fast ships that worked at night) slipped past the Union navy to take out cotton and bring in guns, ammunition, and luxury items for Southern ladies. However, as the war went on the blockade grew stronger and the South began to run out of many important supplies like medicine for wounded soldiers, shoes, and even cloth for uniforms.

The second part of the Union strategy was to capture the Mississippi River. This would stop all trade and travel on this important route for the Confederacy. It would also cut off the eastern states from the states to the west.

The last part of the Union strategy was to divide the Confederacy into smaller parts and capture the capital at Richmond. This strategy eventually won the war. However, due to clever southern generals, valiant Confederate soldiers, and poor Union generals, it took four years of hard fighting to succeed.

 Answer these questions.

1.1   What were the two capitals of the Confederacy? _____

_____

1.2   Who was president of the U.S. when the Confederacy was created?

_____

1.3   What was the name of the compromise that would have protected slavery south of

the Missouri Compromise line? _____

1.4   How and when did the Civil War start? _____

_____

1.5   (Using the map) What were the eleven states of the Confederacy?

_____

_____

_____

1.6   What advantages did the Union have in the Civil War? _____

_____

_____

_____

5

1.7 What advantages did the Confederacy have? _____

_____

_____

1.8 What were the three parts of the Union strategy? _____

_____

_____

1.9 Why did the Confederacy think Britain would help them? _____

_____

1.10 Why didn't Britain help the Confederacy? _____

_____

_____

Before Gettysburg

Commanders. The biggest problem the Union had in the early part of the war was finding a general who could fight and win! Abraham Lincoln had to choose the commander for the Union. He went through no less than six men before he found what he needed in Ulysses S. Grant. Grant was a heavy drinking man who was not brilliant, but went and did what was needed to win. Grant had several capable generals under him. William T. Sherman was the best known general under Grant, and became famous for the destruction he brought to the south. These men brought about the victories Lincoln needed to defeat the Confederacy.

The South had capable commanders from the start. Robert E. Lee was their commander for most of the war and probably the best general on either side. Lee was a brilliant fighter who constantly surprised his enemy with how, when, and where he attacked. He was a soldier in the U.S. army when the war began and moved to the Confederate army when his home state of Virginia seceded. He was aided by General Thomas Jackson who was equally brilliant in battle. Jackson won the nickname "Stonewall" for standing "like a stone wall" in the First Battle of Bull Run.

Bull Run. Both sides were eager for war in 1861. Neither believed the other could or would fight well. However, Irvin McDowell, the first Union commander, wanted time to teach his untrained volunteer troops the skills they needed to fight as an army, but Lincoln and the Union people pushed hard for the new army to go into battle. Even though McDowell thought his army was unprepared, he moved it into Virginia in July 1861.

The first full battle of the war was fought at Bull Run near Washington, D.C. Many people from Washington followed the army out with picnic lunches to watch. The inexperienced Union army was stopped at Bull Run by the inexperienced Confederate army. Eventually, the Union troops panicked and ran when more Southern soldiers arrived. It was a humiliating defeat for the Union.

(NOTE: The Union usually named battles after the nearest water like Bull Run, a creek. The Confederacy named them after the nearest town,

calling Bull Run the Battle of Manassas. Therefore, many Civil War battles have two names. This LIFEPAC will use the Union names.)

After the defeat at Bull Run, General George McClellan was put in command of the Union army. He trained and organized it into a strong fighting force. However, it took months getting the army ready and he still did not want it to go into battle until he thought everything was perfect. Even after months of training, he still resisted leading the army into battle unless he was forced to by orders; even then, they fought **timidly**, retreating quickly. Lincoln got so frustrated with him that he once asked to borrow the army since McClellan wasn't doing anything with it!

McClellan finally moved the army by sea to an area near the James River south of Richmond in the Spring of 1862. He was defeated by General Lee at Fair Oaks and Battles of the Seven Days.

Believing that McClellan would not fight anymore, Lee moved north to Bull Run. McClellan was relieved of his command, but the new Union general, John Pope, was defeated by Jackson and Lee at the second Battle of Bull Run.

McClellan was restored to his command. He made some advances, but assuming he was outnumbered, continued his cautious ways.

Ironclads. The Confederacy did not have a navy to break the Union blockade, but in March of 1862 they tried to break it using an ironclad ship. Ships in the 1860s were usually made of wood. A few ships with iron plates on the outside had been built in Europe, but the Confederate ship *Merrimac* was the first one built in America. It attacked the Union ships guarding Chesapeake Bay destroying two of them and endangering the blockade.

The next day, a newly built Union ironclad ship called the *Monitor* arrived. The two ships met and fought for several hours. It was the first battle in history between ironclad ships. Neither could sink the other, however it was considered a Union victory because the blockade remained.

THE *MERRIMAC* AND THE *MONITOR* IN BATTLE

Emancipation Proclamation. At the start of the war, President Lincoln had been careful to say that he was fighting to save the Union. He tried to make sure that the slave states along the border did not turn to the Confederacy early in the war, so he did not say he was fighting to end slavery, but by late 1862 he decided that the time had come to give the war a new **moral** purpose. However, he wanted to wait and make the announcement after a Union victory, not after all the defeats.

General Lee gave him a chance when the South attacked Maryland in September of 1862. McClellan met Lee at the Battle of Antietam. On that one day, 20,000 Americans, North and South, were killed or wounded. Neither side defeated the other, but Lee retreated the next day. Lincoln used the opportunity to claim a Union victory and made his announcement against slavery.

Lincoln's announcement came on September 22, 1861. It was called the **Emancipation** Proclamation. It granted freedom to all the slaves in the states in the Confederacy after January 1, 1863. It did *not* free the slaves in the border states that were loyal to the Union. It did, however, mean that victory for the Union would mean the end of slavery in the South and the rest of the nation was sure to follow. The Emancipation Proclamation was the beginning of the end of slavery in America.

Complete these sentences.

1.11 The first full battle of the war was at _____ in July of

_____ .

1.12 The Confederate commander for most of the war was _____

and the brilliant general under him was _____ .

1.13 President Lincoln had _____ (how many) commanders before he found

one who could defeat the South.

1.14 The Union general who finally won for the North was _____

who was helped by _____ .

1.15 The _____ won the battles of Fair Oaks, Seven Days and

Second Bull Run.

1.16 The first battle of ironclad ships was between the _____

and the _____ .

1.17 Lincoln's order that freed the slaves in the Confederacy was called the

_____ . It was issued after a Union victory at the

Battle of _____ .

1.18 General _____ organized and trained the Union army

after First Bull Run, but hesitated to use it.

More Confederate Victories. Lincoln finally lost patience with McClellan, who did not chase Lee after Antietam. He put Ambrose Burnside in command. Burnside promptly attacked Lee and lost at the Battle of Fredricksburg in December, 1862. Lincoln changed generals again to General Joseph Hooker who rebuilt the army and attacked Lee in the Spring of 1863 at Chancerlorville. Lee had half as many men as Hooker, yet he won the four-day long battle. However, the South suffered a serious loss when Stonewall Jackson was accidentally shot and killed by his own men.

In the West. The only thing that kept the Union from despair the first year and a half of the war were the victories in the west. General Ulysses S. Grant, in particular, was steadily capturing forts on the Mississippi and railroad **junctions** the South needed to move supplies and men. Grant captured two key forts, Fort Henry and Fort Donelson, near the Tennessee-Kentucky border in February of 1862. He earned the nickname "Unconditional Surrender" Grant when he demanded unconditional surrender from the Southern army at Donelson.

After those victories, Grant moved south to attack a railroad junction at Corinth, Mississippi, but before he could get there, the western Confederate army under General Johnston surprised Grant's army at the Battle of Shiloh in April 1862. This vicious battle left about 24,000 Americans dead or wounded. The Union army eventually won, but at a terrible price. Many people wanted Grant fired because of the huge death toll, but Lincoln would not fire a general who was willing to fight and win.

While the Union army was working its way down the Mississippi from the north, the Union navy was fighting its way north along the same river. Admiral David Farragut captured New Orleans in April of 1862, Baton Rouge in May, and then moved on to take Natchez, Mississippi. By the end of 1862, the fortress city of Vicksburg, Mississippi was one of the few places still in Confederate hands on the Mississippi River.

The city of Vicksburg was on a tall cliff overlooking a bend in the river. From there it could fire on any Union ship trying to travel on it and protect any Confederate ships bringing supplies across from the western states. General Grant could not reach the city from either the west or the north, so he came in from the south and moved to the east side of the city, which was the only flat way into it.

In May of 1863 Grant began a siege of the city. Union cannons bombarded the city around the clock. The women and children of the city moved into caves to survive. Food was hard to find. People ate horses, dogs, and rats. Finally, the Confederate commander realized that he had no chance of victory and surrendered on July 4, 1863. He hoped that surrendering on the nation's birthday would encourage Grant to be kind to the defeated soldiers.

Life in the War. The men in both armies suffered from many difficulties. Food was usually plain, often full of bugs, and the men usually had to cook it themselves. In the South, the army often went hungry because there was no food or no way to get it to the men where they were fighting. The Southern army also suffered from a lack of uniforms, blankets, and shoes during the war. Many of the Confederate soldiers went barefoot and wore **homespun** by the end of the war.

We know today that disease is often

THE VICKSBURG BATTLEFIELD - VIEW FROM *FORT HILL* ON THE NORTH SIDE OF THE CITY, OVERLOOKING THE *MISSISSIPPI RIVER.* INSET: THE CONFEDERATE COURTHOUSE THAT SURRENDERED.

caused and spread by not cleaning wounds, people, and places properly. The people in the 1860s did not know this. Army camps and hospitals were often filthy, dirty places. Disease actually killed more men during the Civil War than bullets did! A serious wound on a leg or an arm often meant that it would be cut off because the doctors could not repair it or prevent an **infection**. The Northern doctors did learn during the war that more men stayed alive in clean places than in dirty ones. However, the South did not have the soap or supplies to clean up its camps, even if they had wanted to.

The soldiers who suffered the most were those captured in battle. Early in the war, the two sides exchanged prisoners. However, that stopped in 1863 when the Union began accepting blacks to fight in the army. Eventually, almost 200,000 black men served honorably in the Union army. However, the South treated captured black soldiers as escaped slaves, not prisoners, and would not exchange them. The Union refused to continue exchanging prisoners unless the black soldiers were also sent back. Ironically, toward the end of the war, the Confederacy drafted black soldiers.

Without exchanges, the prison camps in the North and South quickly became overcrowded. The camps were given very little in the way of food and medicine when so much was needed for the armies. In the south, where the army had so little, the prisoners had less. Thousands of men died in the prison camps.

Most of the men in the Union and Confederate armies were volunteers. However, by the middle of the war both sides needed more men. The Confederacy passed the first draft law in American history in 1862. This was a law forcing some men between the ages of 18 and 35 to join the army. The Union passed a similar law. Both sides allowed men to hire someone to fight in their place or pay a large fee to avoid being drafted. Thus, the rich could avoid the draft while the poor could not. This made many of the poor soldiers angry. There even was a riot against the draft in New York City in 1863.

Name the person, battle, thing or place.

1.19 _____ Two day battle; Johnston surprised Grant; 24,000 Americans hurt or killed

1.20 _____ City taken by siege on the Mississippi; surrendered on July 4, 1863

1.21 _____
_____ Two forts captured by Grant in February 1862

1.22 _____ Admiral who took New Orleans and Baton Rouge

1.23 _____ Losing general at Fredricksburg

1.24 _____ Losing general at Chancerlorville

1.25 _____ Important Southern general killed at Chancerlorville

1.26 _____ Rich men could pay to avoid the army under this law

1.27 _____ The south refused to exchange these soldiers

1.28 _____ This killed more soldiers than bullets

Union Victorious

Gettysburg. Up until July of 1863, the war was going well for the Confederacy, except along the Mississippi. Then, Lee decided to take the war north, hoping to capture Philadelphia and Washington. That might end the war, so he marched his army into Pennsylvania. Lincoln quickly put George Meade, a Pennsylvania general, in command to stop the Confederate army.

On July 1, 1863 a small group of Confederate soldiers came into the town of Gettysburg, Pennsylvania looking for shoes. They met some Union soldiers and fighting began. Both sides sent for help and more soldiers quickly arrived. Meade and the Union army fought from a hill called Cemetery Ridge south of the town. Lee tried to drive them out in a three day battle.

Photos (except right) by R. Scott Dann

GETTYSBURG, PENNSYLVANIA
TOP: THE HILL PICKETT CHARGED. LEFT: A UNION CANNON.
MIDDLE: THE VIRGINIA MEMORIAL. RIGHT: GENERAL LEE'S HEADQUARTERS.

The Confederates suffered huge losses sending men up the hill to attack the Union army. On the last day of the battle, Lee ordered General George Pickett to attack straight up the hill with more than 13,000 men. The Union army blanketed the enemy with rifle and cannon fire. The few Confederate soldiers that survived to reach the top were immediately captured. Lee was forced to retreat. Meade then made the same mistake the other Union generals had made. He did not follow and Lee escaped to fight another day.

Neither side knew it, but Gettysburg was the turning point of the war. The South had been mainly winning up until Gettysburg, at least in the east. After Gettysburg they would usually lose.

The Union built a cemetery at Gettysburg for the dead from both sides. It was dedicated in November, 1863. Abraham Lincoln spoke briefly at the dedication. He spoke of the American dream of liberty and equality. He urged Americans to live up to that dream and fight for the freedom promised by their nation. He said, "...We here...resolve that...government of the people, by the people, for the people, shall not perish from this earth." Although short, the *Gettysburg Address* was President Lincoln's most famous speech.

Tennessee. The Union army captured Chattanooga, a railroad junction in September 1863. The Confederate army won its last victory outside the city at Chickamauga a few days later. Then, the Southern army laid siege to the city to drive the Yankees out of it, but General Grant was put in command in the west. He saved the city and drove the Confederate army out of Tennessee.

Grant in Command. Seeing his many victories, Lincoln put Ulysses S. Grant in command of the entire Union army in March of 1864. Grant put William T. Sherman in command of the army in Tennessee and ordered him to capture Atlanta in northwest Georgia. Sherman took the city in August of 1864. In November, he destroyed it and marched his army south to Savannah. Along the way, he and his army stole or destroyed anything that might help the Confederate cause: crops, homes, railroads, and animals. Sherman's army left a 60 mile wide path of

11

destruction across Georgia. The Confederacy did not have anyone who could stop Sherman's *March to the Sea.* Sherman's March was a bitter memory for the South for many, many years.

Grant, in the meantime, moved into Virginia to chase Lee. The two met at yet another bloody battle at the Wilderness in May of 1864. Neither side won, but Grant kept coming. He pushed Lee back to Petersburg which was a very important railroad junction near Richmond. There Lee's army stayed to defend the city. Grant set up a siege. The two sides fought there until the weakened Confederate army could not hold any longer.

In the meantime, Sherman captured Savannah and marched north to take the capitals of South and North Carolina. He continued to destroy everything in his path. The Union also held an election in November of 1864 and re-elected Abraham Lincoln with Andrew Johnson, a loyal Tennessee Democrat, as vice president. Lincoln had held the nation together and kept the war going for four long years. Now the end was finally near.

Lee retreated from Petersburg in April of 1865. Grant chased him and cut off his escape route. Finally, Lee sent a message asking to meet and discuss terms of surrender. Generals Grant and Lee met in the small town of Appomattox Courthouse, Virginia to arrange the surrender. Grant was very generous. The Confederate soldiers were given food, allowed to keep their horses for farming, and set free if they turned in their weapons. Even Lee and his officers were set free and allowed to keep their pistols. The surrender of Lee on April 12, 1865 was the end of the Confederacy. There was a little more fighting, but the remaining armies surrendered within a month. The Union was whole again.

 **Answer these questions.**

1.29 What was the last Confederate victory? _____

1.30 Which Confederate general led the charge up Cemetery Ridge on the last day of the

Battle of Gettysburg? _____

1.31 Who was the Union commander at Gettysburg? _____

1.32 What was President Lincoln's most famous speech?

_____

1.33 Where did General Lee surrender? _____

1.34 Who was elected president in 1864? _____

Vice-president? _____

1.35 What battle was the turning point of the Civil War? _____

1.36 What was the name of General Sherman's march from Atlanta to Savannah?

_____

1.37 What did Sherman do on that march? _____

_____

1.38 Who did Lincoln put in command of the Union army in March of 1864?

_____

1.39 What were the generous terms given to the Confederate soldiers when Lee

surrendered? _____

_____

_____

_____

Review the material in this section in preparation for the Self Test. The Self Test will check
your mastery of this particular section. The items missed on this Self Test will
indicate specific areas where restudy is needed for mastery.

SELF TEST 1

Match these people (each answer, 3 points).

1.01 _____ Became the Union commander after winning
victories in the west

1.02 _____ Organized the Union army but was slow and
timid about going into battle

1.03 _____ Was president when the first 7 states seceded

1.04 _____ Tennessee Democrat, elected vice president

1.05 _____ Admiral who captured New Orleans

1.06 _____ Union general who destroyed all in his path on
his March to the Sea

1.07 _____ President of the U.S. during the Civil War

1.08 _____ President of the Confederacy

1.09 _____ Commander of the Confederate army

1.010 _____ Confederate general accidentally killed by his own men

a. Abraham Lincoln

b. Ulysses S. Grant

c. George McClellan

d. Robert E. Lee

e. Stonewall Jackson

f. William T. Sherman

g. James Buchanan

h. Jefferson Davis

i. Andrew Johnson

j. David Farragut

Choose the correct place or battle from the list (each answer, 3 points).

Gettysburg   Fort Sumter   Bull Run

Vicksburg   Antietam   Shiloh

Appomattox Courthouse   Chickamauga   Atlanta

Petersburg

1.011 _____ The Union lost two battles here, Washington citizens
brought picnics to the first one

1.012 _____ Sherman took this city and then destroyed it

1.013 _____ Lee attacked into Maryland, twenty thousand Americans
killed or injured, Lee retreated, Lincoln used the victory to
announce freedom for the slaves

1.014 _____ Lee surrendered

1.015 _____ Turning point of the war, Meade won in Pennsylvania,
Pickett's charge failed to take Cemetery Ridge

1.016 _____ Grant pushed Lee back until the Southern army stopped to defend a railroad junction near Richmond

1.017 _____ General Grant laid siege to this fortress city on the Mississippi, it surrendered on the 4th of July

1.018 _____ Last battle won by the Confederacy

1.019 _____ Started the Civil War, Confederates bombarded a Union post in the south

1.020 _____ The Union army was surprised by the Confederates under Johnston; 24,000 Americans were killed or wounded

Answer these questions (each answer, 4 points).

1.021 What was unusual about the battle between the *Monitor* and the *Merrimac*?

_____

_____

_____

1.022 What was the Emancipation Proclamation?

_____

_____

_____

1.023 What was the Crittenden Compromise?

_____

_____

_____

1.024 What were the generous terms of surrender given to the Southern army?

_____

_____

_____

1.025 Why didn't Britain help the Confederacy?

_____

_____

_____

Put an "N" if the statement is true for the North, an "S" for the South, and a "B" for both (each answer, 2 points).

1.026 _____ Had more men and factories

1.027 _____ Army food was plain and often full of bugs

1.028 _____ Had a large navy

1.029 _____ Had more railroads

1.030 _____ Planned to capture the Mississippi

1.031 _____ A blockade caused them great problems with supplies

1.032 _____ Prison camps were overcrowded by the end of the war

1.033 _____ Used black soldiers

1.034 _____ Would win if they only survived

1.035 _____ Had trouble finding generals who could win victories

Score
Teacher Check _____
Initial   **Date**

II. RECONSTRUCTION

The Union was whole again after Appomattox Courthouse. But, was it really? The south did not want to be part of the Union. It would not cooperate in freeing the slaves and making them citizens. Much of the south was in ruins and its people had no money to rebuild. The leaders of the United States had a huge job to rebuild the south, set up laws to protect the newly freed slaves (freedmen), create new state governments and convince the south to accept being a part of the nation again. Unfortunately, the one man who might have been able to do these things died just as the war ended. Without Abraham Lincoln, the Reconstruction of the south was largely a nasty mess.

Review these objectives. When you have completed this section, you should be able to:

3. Describe the course of Reconstruction and its major events.
4. Name the contents of the Thirteenth, Fourteenth, and Fifteenth Amendments to the Constitution.

Restudy these words.

bond	comedy	contract
corrupt	scandal	tactless

Presidential Reconstruction

Lincoln's Assassination. Abraham Lincoln had been a great president. He had kept the Union fighting through a difficult, bloody war. He had freed the slaves. He wanted to put the nation back together as peacefully and kindly as possible. He was good at working with people and convincing them to work with him. He might have been able to build a fair and successful way to put the north and south back together. However, he never had the chance.

On April 14, 1865 Lincoln and his wife went to see a play, a **comedy**, at Ford's Theater. He wanted to relax after the good news of Lee's surrender two days earlier. He did not know that John Wilkes Booth, an actor who wanted revenge for the defeat of

PRESIDENT ABRAHAM LINCOLN

the south, was planning to kill him there. Booth snuck up behind Lincoln during the play and shot him in the back of the head. Then, he jumped from the Lincolns' balcony seat onto the stage, breaking his leg. He shouted at the stunned crowd and ran out the back of the building where he had a horse waiting.

Abraham Lincoln was taken to a house across the street where he died the next morning. Booth fled, chased by federal troops. The soldiers eventually cornered him in a barn and killed him.

The assassination stunned the north. They had been angry at the south, now the anger grew deeper. The Republican leaders of Congress wanted revenge and Lincoln was no longer there to stop them. Lincoln's assassination meant the south lost the one person in Washington who might have been able to help them. Now, the south would have to face the anger of the Union without any protection.

Andrew Johnson. Andrew Johnson became president when Lincoln died. He was a Democrat from Tennessee. Because the election took place during the war, Lincoln wanted a Democratic running mate to unite the country. Now, Johnson, who was stubborn and **tactless**, was president. He did not have Lincoln's sense of humor, way with people, or popularity. He would fight with the Republican Congress about how to manage the south and he would lose.

Johnson's Plan. Johnson decided to use a plan Lincoln had set up before he died. It was called the *Ten Percent Plan*. Under it, the southern states could form a new government when ten percent of the citizens had taken an oath of loyalty to the United States. The new state government would have to approve the Thirteenth Amendment to the Constitution (which ended slavery) and refuse to pay the money owed to the old Confederate governments. Then, the state could send representatives to Washington and rejoin the Union.

The southern states quickly fulfilled these easy terms. However, many of the men

PRESIDENT ANDREW JOHNSON

they sent to Congress had been important people in the Confederate army and government. One of the new Congressmen had even been the vice president of the Confederacy! The new southern governments also passed *Black Codes* that restricted the rights of the new freedmen so severely that they were almost slaves again!

Radical Republicans. The Republicans who controlled Congress were furious. They had fought a war to free the slaves and now it was as if they had lost, not won. They wanted the south punished for the Civil War. Also, the Republicans during the war had controlled Congress. They had passed many new laws that increased the tariff, gave land to build railroads in the north, and gave free land to settlers in the west. They did not want the southern Congressmen, who were mainly Democrats, to change what they had done.

So, the Republican Congress refused to let the new southern Congressmen take their jobs in Washington. (The Constitution allows Congress to do that in Article I,

Section V.1). They also refused to allow the Confederate States to rejoin the Union. Then, under the leadership of Representative Thaddeus Stevens, a man deeply committed to the rights of black Americans, a group called the "Radical Republicans" took matters into their own hands. They set up the Joint (House and Senate) Committee on Reconstruction and began to work on their own plans.

Congress began by passing the first Civil Rights Act in 1866 to stop some of the abuses of the Black Codes. It protected the rights of black people as American citizens. Johnson vetoed the law but Congress overrode the veto. Then, Congress passed the Fourteenth Amendment to the Constitution which gave the freedmen the rights of citizens and punished states that did not let them vote. It was sent to the states for approval.

The southern states refused to ratify (accept) the Fourteenth Amendment. Johnson, who would not compromise on his plan, went on a tour of the north trying to convince people to vote against the Radical Republicans in the 1866 election. However, the Republicans won the election by a large majority. They gained control of more than two-thirds of the seats in both the House and the Senate. That meant they could override any veto by Johnson. When the new Congress came to Washington in March of 1867, they were determined to run things their way now.

 Complete these sentences.

2.1   Lincoln was assassinated by _____ at

        _____ .

2.2   Andrew Johnson's Reconstruction plan was called the _____

        _____ .

2.3   The laws passed in the south that almost made the Freedman slaves again were called the _____ .

2.4   The men in Congress who wanted to punish the South were called the

        _____ .

2.5   Congress passed the first _____ in 1866 to protect the freedman.

2.6   The _____ Amendment gave freedmen citizenship and punished states that did not let them vote.

2.7   The _____ Amendment ended slavery in America.

2.8   _____ was the leader of the the Republicans in Congress who opposed Johnson's plan.

Radical Reconstruction

Life in the South. The war had destroyed the south. The few factories were not working. The plantation owners had lost their workers and did not have money for seeds or horses to pull plows. All of the wealth of the Confederacy was gone. The government **bonds** were no good and neither was the money. The former rich aristocrats were poor and very bitter.

The end of slavery was a shock to the south. Millions of freedmen were suddenly pulled out of the only life they knew. They were free, but they had no education, no job skills, and no money. The Freedmen's Bureau was set up to teach them to read and figure, give them food and clothing, and give them government land. The Bureau did teach many of the former slaves to read. However, it was not able to get land for them. Most blacks were forced to take low paying city jobs or work for their former masters as sharecroppers. Sharecroppers raised crops on a piece of land and paid rent by giving the owner part of the crop.

Military Occupation. Congress took control of Reconstruction in 1867. This was called *Radical* or *Congressional Reconstruction*. Tennessee, which had ratified the Fourteenth Amendment, was readmitted to the Union. The other ten states of the south were divided into five military districts, each under the command of a Union general. Federal troops were put in the south to force obedience. Most of the former Confederate leaders were denied the right to vote or hold office.

The path to rejoining the Union was also set up by Congress. Election boards were organized to approve voters. All adult black men and certain whites were registered. Each state had to write a constitution that protected the rights of black people to vote. The new state governments also had to approve the Fourteenth Amendment. Then, the state could be readmitted to the Union.

Finally, Congress also approved the Fifteenth Amendment to the Constitution.

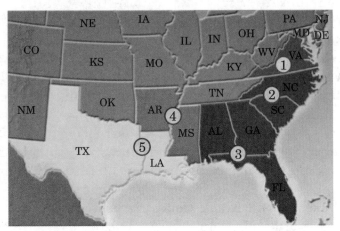

MAP OF THE FIVE MILITARY DISTRICTS

That amendment protected the right of black men to vote in the whole United States. It was ratified in 1870, the last of the "Civil War Amendments."

Carpetbaggers and Scalawags. The new rules gave the vote to thousands of freed slaves who knew nothing about politics. They voted as they were told to vote by the people who had freed them, the Republicans. Most white southerners refused to participate in this new Reconstruction plan. As a result, governments came to power in the south that were made up mainly of carpetbaggers, scalawags, and freedmen. Carpetbaggers were men who came from the north. (They got their name from southerners who believed they had come south in a hurry to get rich, bringing their things in an easily carried carpetbag.) Scalawags were southern people who worked with the new governments. Most southern whites hated carpetbaggers and scalawags, but they especially hated the freedmen who had once been their property.

By 1870, all of the former Confederate states were back in the Union, many of them with Republican state governments. However, these governments could only stay in power by making sure most southern whites did not vote and most southern blacks did. To make matters worse, many of the officeholders were **corrupt**. They were

HISTORY & GEOGRAPHY

5 0 5

LIFEPAC TEST

Name _____

Date _____

Score _____

Possible Score _____ 100

Match these items (each answer, 2 points).

1. _____ Seward's Icebox, purchased for $7.2 million

2. _____ The Confederate army surrendered

3. _____ Southerner who worked with the Reconstruction governments

4. _____ Civil service reform

5. _____ Made the freed blacks almost slaves again

6. _____ Business that controls all sales of one product

7. _____ Confederate stronghold on the Mississippi, taken by a Union siege

8. _____ Began the Civil War

9. _____ Ended slavery in all of America

10. _____ Announcement freeing the Confederate slaves

11. _____ Law to control the railroads

12. _____ Helped former slaves to start new lives

13. _____ Gave 160 acres to someone who lived on it for five years

14. _____ Fought in the first battle of ironclad ships

15. _____ Granted all black men the right to vote

16. _____ The president's plan for Reconstruction

17. _____ Tax loved by industrialists, hated by farmers

18. _____ Turning point of the Civil War

19. _____ Person who paid to rent land by giving the owner part of his crop

20. _____ Company that controlled almost all oil production in the United States

a. Fort Sumter

b. *Monitor*

c. Ten Percent

d. Alaska

e. Homestead Act

f. Gettysburg

g. Sharecropper

h. Scalawag

i. Freedmen's Bureau

j. Black Codes

k. Thirteenth Amendment

l. Fifteenth Amendment

m. Standard Oil

n. Tariff

o. Trust

p. Interstate Commerce Act

q. Pendleton Act

r. Vicksburg

s. Appomattox Courthouse

t. Emancipation Proclamation

Name the person (each answer, 2 points).

21. _____ President during the Civil War, freed the slaves

22. _____ Marched to the Sea, Union general

23. _____ Steel manufacturer, retired to give away his fortune

B

24. _____ President who favored easy Reconstruction, impeached

25. _____ Commander of the Confederate army

26. _____ Inventor of the telephone

27. _____ Radical Republican leader in Congress

28. _____ Made his fortune by controlling oil in America

29. _____ Victorious Union general, bad president

30. _____ Assassinated Abraham Lincoln

Answer these questions (each answer, 4 points).

31. How did Thomas Edison approach inventing?

_____

_____

_____

32. What advantages did the Union have in the Civil War?

_____

_____

_____

33. How did southern whites regain control towards the end of Reconstruction?

_____

_____

_____

34. Why was Seward's Folly not a folly?

_____

_____

_____

35. What was wrong with the civil service during the Gilded Age?

_____

_____

_____

Write *true* **or** *false* **on the blank** (each answer, 2 points).

36. _____ The Confederacy won most of the battles in the east early in the Civil War.

37. _____ The south voted only for the Democratic Party for many years after Reconstruction.

38. _____ Britain joined the Confederacy to fight the Union.

39. _____ Corruption was common in American business and government after the Civil War.

40. _____ During the Gilded Age, many reforms were successful in controlling the corruption of railroads and other businesses.

41. _____ The Crittenden Compromise tried to prevent the split between the Union and the Confederacy by protecting slavery south of the Missouri Compromise line.

42. _____ Immigrants before 1880 usually came from northern Europe.

43. _____ During Congressional Reconstruction the ten southern states that did not approve the 14th Amendment were divided into five military districts under the command of a Union general.

44. _____ After the Civil War, American industry became more valuable than farming.

45. _____ Civil War prison camps overflowed because prisoner exchanges ended when the South would not return black Union soldiers.

RECONSTRUCTION AFTER THE *CIVIL WAR*. ON THE LEFT: *LINCOLN* AND THE *EMANCIPATION PROCLAMATION*.

men out to steal as much government money as they could. This was true all over the U.S. after the Civil War, but it was especially obvious in the south. Southern states lost thousands of dollars to dishonest officials during Radical Reconstruction. This made the white southerners even more bitter. Most southern whites refused to support the new governments and vowed to drive them out of office.

Impeachment. Andrew Johnson had vetoed all of the new Reconstruction laws, but Congress had overridden him each time. Eventually, the leaders of Congress decided they wanted to get rid of Johnson. They had a simple plan. They passed a law they knew he would break. Once he had broken it they would impeach him for "high crimes and misdemeanors" and remove him from office.

The law they passed was called the *Tenure in Office Act*. It made it illegal for the president to fire anyone in his own cabinet. Presidents had always been free to fire their cabinet members before that. As the Radical Republicans had expected, Johnson fired a cabinet member who was working against him. The House immediately impeached him.

The impeachment trial was held in the Senate in 1868. It was a big show. Johnson was extremely unpopular and most people expected him to lose. The Senate even issued tickets that allowed people to come and watch the event.

It was clear from the testimony at the trial that Johnson's only crime was that he disagreed with Congress and was stubborn about it. Nevertheless, more than two-thirds of the senators were Republican, so the Radicals thought they could get the votes they needed to remove Johnson. However, the case against him was so bad that seven of the Republicans voted against impeachment. As a result, Johnson remained president by one vote.

This was an important vote. If Johnson had been removed from office, it might have been dangerous for the country. Congress might have believed it could remove a president any time it did not like him. Future presidents would have to be careful not to make Congress mad, even when it was wrong. But, the vote went in Johnson's favor and the law is that presidents can only be removed if they actually commit "high crimes and misdemeanors."

The Civil War Amendments
13th: Ended slavery
14th: Gave freedmen the rights of citizens
15th: Gave black men the right to vote

Write *true* or *false* in the blank.

2.9 _____ Carpetbaggers were southern people who worked with the Radical Reconstruction governments.

2.10 _____ Radical Reconstruction was under the control of the president.

2.11 _____ The Freedmen's Bureau gave land to most of the former slaves.

2.12 _____ Sharecroppers paid to use land by giving the owner some of the crop they raised.

2.13 _____ The southern states were not readmitted to the Union until they ratified the Fourteenth Amendment.

2.14 _____ The Fourteenth Amendment freed the slaves.

2.15 _____ Andrew Johnson was removed from office by the Senate.

2.16 _____ Many of the Radical Reconstruction governments in the south were corrupt.

2.17 _____ Most southern whites did not support the Radical Reconstruction governments.

2.18 _____ The Fifteenth Amendment protected the right of black men to vote.

2.19 _____ The Tenure in Office Act required the president to appoint men the Senate named to his cabinet.

2.20 _____ During Radical Reconstruction, Republican governments were supported mainly by freed black voters.

2.21 _____ Scalawags were Union soldiers who took jobs in the south.

Corruption

Cheating after the War. The time after the Civil War was full of corruption. The needs of the war created a great deal of waste and many dishonest people were able to cheat the government because the officials were too busy to check anything. Unfortunately, this attitude of "cheat to get what you want" continued and grew worse after the war ended. A large number of judges took bribes to decide lawsuits. Officials took bribes to give men **contracts** to do jobs for the government. Businessmen cheated the people who invested money in their factories and railroads.

The railroads were especially bad. A railroad gave a town or state a great way to ship goods and earn money by trade. So, towns and states paid huge bribes in money and land to convince the railroads to build in their location. Railroads paid bribes to keep the officials from investigating how they did business. The railroads also paid

22

money to get large companies to ship on their trains. Then, they overcharged small businesses and farmers to ship their goods because they had no way to fight back.

Grant as President. A presidential election was held in 1868. Ulysses S. Grant, the victorious Union general, ran as a Republican and won comfortably. Grant, however, was a very poor president. He was an honest man, but he had many dishonest friends, whom he trusted too much. Moreover, the Republican party was working closely with the corrupt businesses. Grant listened to the party leaders and did not try to force changes. He also agreed not to change the way the south was being treated. The Republicans wanted to keep the southern Democrats out of office and they were using harsh Reconstruction plans to do just that.

Scandals. A series of **scandals** bombarded the public during the eight years President Grant was in office. One involved the railroad which was building tracks across the country. The officers of the Union Pacific Railway hired *their own* company, Crédit Mobilier, to do the work and charged almost twice as much as building the track actually cost. To make sure the government did not interfere, several congressmen and the vice president were given stock in Crédit Mobilier to share in the sky high profits.

There were several more scandals. Two wealthy men paid a bribe to President Grant's brother-in-law when they tried to buy up most of the gold in the country in 1869. In the *Whiskey Ring* scandal, several of Grant's officials took bribes from whiskey manufacturers to allow them not to pay taxes on their goods. Grant's secretary of war was impeached in 1876 for taking bribes from businessmen cheating the Indians. Thus, a very good general proved to be a very poor president.

Democrats Return in the South. The white people of the south were almost all Democrats. They slowly began to regain control in the south and get rid of the

PRESIDENT ULYSSES S. GRANT

Republican carpetbaggers and scalawags in office. The main way they did this was by using violence against the black people who were voting for the Republicans.

Southerners formed secret groups, like the Ku Klux Klan, that went out at night to threaten blacks who voted. They would beat, abuse, and kill black men who dared to vote, claim their rights as citizens, or oppose white Democrats. As a result, the freedmen stopped voting and the Democrats returned to power across the south. By 1877, the south was solidly Democratic and it would vote only for the Democratic Party for many, many years.

The north was getting tired of the cost of Reconstruction and very few northerners really cared about the rights of black people, so very little was done as the south took away those rights. Until the Civil Rights Movement of the 1960s, black people in the south would not be treated as full citizens. They were rarely allowed to vote. They had separate schools, public bathrooms, and places at public events that were never as good as those reserved for white people. The state courts would not give them justice and the federal government would not help them. The Civil War gave them freedom, but little else.

End of Reconstruction. The election of 1876 was one of the messiest in American history. The Democratic candidate, Samuel Tilden, probably won, but Rutherford B. Hayes, the Republican, became president. The problem was that the two parties had different results for four states, three of them from the south. The Democrats said Tilden won in those states, while the Republicans said Hayes won. A committee was set up that had 8 Republicans and 7 Democrats to decide who had won. The committee voted 8 to 7 that Hayes had won.

The Democrats threatened to not accept the results. They fought over it so hard that just one month before the president was to be inaugurated, they still hadn't decided who would be president! Finally, the two sides agreed to the *Compromise of 1877.* Hayes became president and, in exchange, the last federal soldiers were removed from the south, ending Reconstruction.

Answer these questions.

2.22   What was wrong with the way people did business and ran the government after the Civil War? _____

_____

2.23   Why was Grant considered a bad president? _____

_____

_____

2.24   What was the Compromise of 1877? _____

_____

_____

2.25   How did the white Democrats regain control in the south? _____

_____

_____

2.26   Why was there a problem about the election of 1876? _____

_____

_____

2.27   What was the Crédit Mobilier Scandal? _____

_____

_____

What was the Whisky Ring Scandal? _____

_____

Review the material in this section in preparation for the Self Test. The Self Test will check your mastery of this particular section and the previous section. The items missed on this Self Test will indicate specific areas where restudy is needed for mastery.

SELF TEST 2

Match these people (each answer, 2 points).

2.01 _____ Confederate general

2.02 _____ President who ended Reconstruction

2.03 _____ Civil War president, assassinated

2.04 _____ Congressman who led in harsh Reconstruction of the south

2.05 _____ Poor president, many scandals

2.06 _____ President of the Confederacy

2.07 _____ Union admiral, captured New Orleans

2.08 _____ Union general, good organizer, poor fighter

2.09 _____ Union general, marched to the sea in Georgia destroying everything in his path

2.010 _____ President, impeached for opposing Congress

a. Abraham Lincoln

b. Ulysses S. Grant

c. Andrew Johnson

d. Thadeus Stevens

e. Rutherford B. Hayes

f. William T. Sherman

g. Robert E. Lee

h. Jefferson Davis

i. David Farragut

j. George McClellan

Complete these sentences (each answer, 3 points).

2.011 The Congressmen who wanted to treat the south harshly were the _____ Republicans.

2.012 Andrew Johnson's plan for Reconstruction was the _____ Plan.

2.013 Under Johnson's Reconstruction plan, the southern states passed strict laws called _____ that made the freedmen almost slaves again.

2.014 The _____ Amendment ended slavery.

2.015 A _____ in the south paid for renting land by giving the owner part of the crop he raised.

2.016 _____ were men from the north who came south and took jobs in the government during Reconstruction.

2.017 After Reconstruction, the south voted only for the _____ Party for many, many years.

2.018 The Civil War began when the Confederacy fired on _____ .

2.019   The Battle of _____ was the turning point of the Civil War.

2.020   During the harsh Reconstruction, the 10 states that refused the Fourteenth Amendment were divided into five military districts under the command of a

_____ .

2.021   _____ were southerners who worked with the Reconstruction governments.

2.022   The White people of the south regained control of their governments during Reconstruction by using violence to stop _____ from voting.

2.023   The _____ Amendment gave black men the right to vote.

2.024   The first battle of ironclad ships was between the _____ and the _____ in the Civil War.

2.025   The _____ by Abraham Lincoln freed the slaves in the Confederacy during the Civil War.

2.026   During the Civil War, the _____ had more men, factories, and railroads.

2.027   The _____ Bureau tried to educate the newly freed slaves in the south and help them get started in their new lives.

2.028   In the early part of the Civil War in the east, the _____ won most of the battles.

2.029   Lee surrendered at _____ .

Answer *true* **or** *false* (each answer, 2 points).

2.030   _____ Most southern people agreed with the harsh Reconstruction governments.

2.031   _____ John Wilkes Booth assassinated Ulysses S. Grant.

2.032   _____ Congress would not allow the Confederate states to rejoin the Union under Andrew Johnson's Reconstruction plan.

2.033   _____ Many of the southern state governments under Congressional Reconstruction were Republican.

2.034   _____ There was a great deal of corruption in government and business after the Civil War.

2.035 _____ After Reconstruction, black Americans in the south were not treated as full citizens until the Civil Rights movement of the 1960s.

2.036 _____ When General Lee surrendered, General Grant was very harsh toward him and the Confederate army.

2.037 _____ Britain refused to join the Confederacy in fighting the Union.

2.038 _____ During the Civil War, prisoner exchanges were stopped because the South would not return black soldiers.

2.039 _____ The Compromise of 1877 was an agreement on Reconstruction between Congress and President Johnson

III. THE GILDED AGE

The time after Reconstruction until the 1900s was called the *Gilded Age*. It was a time of the Wild West, the end of the frontier, growing industries, incredibly wealthy businessmen, very poor immigrants, corruption, and calls for reforms. The country was finally united after years of conflict and war over slavery, but it was divided differently, by money and power. New inventions and industries changed the nation. America grew into a world power and in the years after 1890 would begin to act like one.

Review these objectives. When you have completed this section, you should be able to:

5. Describe life in the Gilded Age in America.
6. Explain how the railroad and Homestead Act encouraged settlement of the Great Plains.
7. Name some of the key people of the era and their accomplishments.
8. Describe some of the problems of the Gilded Age and the attempts to correct them.

Restudy these words.

corporation	dominate	epidemic
lavish	pension	ruthless
slum		

Frontier's End

Alaska. Russia had owned Alaska since the 1700s. In 1867, the Russian government sold it to the United States for $7.2 million, or about 2¢ an acre. Many people thought it was a complete waste of money to buy this huge, cold northern land that could never be farmed. They were angry with William Seward, the secretary of state who arranged the sale. They called the land "Seward's Folly" or "Seward's Icebox." Years later, the state proved its worth by becoming a valuable source of fish, wood, oil, and minerals.

Very few people except Native Americans lived in Alaska until the 1880s. Then, miners found gold near what is now the city of Juneau in 1880. More was discovered in the Klondike, in Canada near Alaska, in 1896. Still more gold was discovered in other parts of the territory in 1898 and 1902. These discoveries brought gold rushes and settlers, bringing the territory's population above 60,000 by 1900. However, America's last frontier would not become a state until 1959.

Railroads. Alaska became America's last frontier because the rest of the frontier was filling up with people. The main cause of this inflow of people was the expanding railroad. The first *transcontinental railroad* (one that runs all the way across the continent) was finished in 1869. This opened up easy access to the land between California and the east.

Before the Civil War, the U.S. government had wanted a transcontinental railroad to allow speedy trade and communication with the state of California. However, the northern Congressmen wanted it in the north and the southern Congressmen insisted it had to be in the south. As a result, it was not begun until the Civil War.

During the Civil War, the southern Congressmen were not in Congress to argue the point. So, the route chosen went west from Omaha, Nebraska to Sacramento, California. The government offered large loans and land to encourage the railroad to be built quickly.

Two companies were chosen to do the building. Each was given twenty square miles of land near the tracks for every mile of track they laid. The Central Pacific built east from Sacramento while the Union Pacific built west from Omaha. The job immediately became a race. Each company wanted to build more track to get more of the land and money.

The Union Pacific had easier work building on the flat prairie. They built 1,086 miles of track during the seven year race. The Central Pacific, which had to go through the mountains, managed to build only 689 miles in the same time. The two sides met near Ogden, Utah in May, 1869. There, a ceremony was held and a gold spike was driven in to hold down the very last piece of track.

Four more railways across the nation were built in the next thirty years. Miles of track were laid connecting them to cities and towns all over the country. This brought easy access to the farmland, ranch land, and mines of the west. People flocked to the west, filling up the empty lands. Soon, the frontier was gone, replaced by farms, towns and businesses.

Wild West. The west was a wild place in those years after the Civil War. Towns grew quickly, often with very little law and order. Outlaws took advantage of the open west and hid in the rugged mountains and empty spaces. The crush of incoming people threatened the land of the Plains Indians

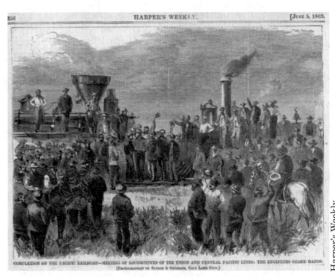

"The Driving of the Last Spike"

who fought back in a series of wars, which they eventually lost. Mining towns grew up in weeks when gold or silver was discovered and died as quickly when the treasure was gone, leaving ghost towns. This was also the time of the big cattle drives that made the American cowboy so famous.

The cattle drives began in the 1870s because ranchers in Texas had huge herds of cattle and the railroads in the north provided a way to transport the cattle east. The ranchers would raise the cattle on the open grassland in Texas. When they were nice and fat, cowboys would slowly herd them north across the open prairie to the railroad along one of the long cattle trails. At the railroad towns, the cattle were put on the trains and shipped east for slaughter and sale to the eastern cities. It was a very profitable business.

These cattle drives made the American cowboy famous in the east. The herds often included thousands of cows and the drives lasted weeks. Cowboys had to be good at riding horses, catching runaways, roping, and shooting (to protect the herd from Indians and thieves). Stories of their long, lonely trips across the open land became popular in the east, making the cowboy a part of American **folklore**.

Homesteads. The long cattle drives only lasted about 20 years. Too many people got into the business and the price of cattle began to go down. Bad winters killed off many of the animals. However, the biggest problem was that the open grasslands the herds had to cross were being fenced. People were moving west and farming the land under the Homestead Act, so the cattle could not cross it freely.

The U.S. government owned millions of acres of land in the Great Plains after the Mexican War (1846-48). Like most government land, it was for sale to settlers, but this land was flat and dry—very different from the farmland of the east. Most Americans were not willing to risk their money on such land. During the Civil War, the U.S. Congress decided to give the land to people who were willing to settle it. They did this with the Homestead Act.

The Homestead Act gave 160 acres of land to any American citizen who would live and work on it for five years. At the end of five years, the land belonged to them. This law was an incredible success. By 1900 about 80 million acres of land had been given away. Even more was sold by the railroads and other people who had bought large tracts to make a profit. As a result, the territories in the Great Plains filled up rapidly after the Civil War. Nine new states were added in the west between the Civil War and 1900.

A "HOMESTEADER" FAMILY

Life on a Great Plains homestead was very difficult. Wood was scarce, so homes were built out of chunks of grass and dirt called sod. These sod houses were dark and dirty, but good shelter. Homes were often far apart, so loneliness was a problem. Doctors were rare. Violent thunderstorms and tornadoes would destroy years of work. Grasshoppers would come in huge clouds some years to eat every living plant in their path. Many of the families gave up and left. However, enough stayed to eventually spread out across the west and fill up the once empty land.

 Name the person, place or thing.

3.1 _____ Seward's Icebox

3.2 _____ Completed near Ogden, Utah in 1869

3.3 _____ Made the American cowboy famous

3.4 _____ Gave a citizen 160 acres of land for living on it five years

3.5 _____ Company that built the first transcontinental railroad west from Omaha

3.6 _____ Company that built east from California

3.7 _____ Amount the U.S. paid for Alaska

3.8 _____ Used by Homesteaders to build houses on the Great Plains

3.9 _____ Used by people to go west and fill up the frontier quickly

3.10 _____ Mineral that brought a rush of settlers to Alaska

3.11 _____ Cattle were driven north to reach this

3.12 _____ Used to hold down the last piece of track on the transcontinental railroad

---

Growth of Industry and Wealth

Changes. America had been founded by people looking for freedom and their own land to farm. Farming had always been the most important business in the United States. However, that changed after the Civil War. Manufacturing had been increasing in America for years. The War of 1812 had given it a big push, but it was the Civil War and the railroads that pushed it over the top. In the 1890s manufacturing became more valuable than farming for the nation and that has been true ever since. America, after the Civil War, became an industrial power.

Railroads. Part of the change in America after the Civil War was that manufacturing businesses got much bigger. Factories used to be small, owned by a man or a family. After the Civil War, they became huge, owned by many men who invested money to build them. They became bigger, faster, made better products, and sold them cheaper than ever before. They were run by **corporations**. The railroads were the first major corporations in the new way of doing business.

Building and running railroads took a huge amount of money. Money was needed for tracks, engines, cars, and workers. Workers were needed to build the tracks, repair them, run the trains, sell tickets, load cargo, and many other things. One man could not afford to pay for all those things, so many men put their money together and made a corporation. These corporations were worth millions of dollars and the profits made hundreds of men very wealthy. Cornelius Vanderbilt and Leland Stanford were among the many men who made vast fortunes in the railroad business.

Other Businesses. Steel also became a big business after the Civil War. Steel rails were better than iron for the railroads and the metal had many other uses in industry. A new way of making steel called the Bessemer Process, made it cheaper than before the war. In the United States, the most well-known name in the steel industry was Andrew Carnegie.

Andrew Carnegie came to America from Scotland as a poor immigrant. He started working when he was 12 at a cotton mill. He worked hard and found ways to get better and better jobs. He also invested his money wisely. He realized in the 1870s that steel would be a good investment. America had all of the resources needed to make steel and the Bessemer Process allowed the steel to be manufactured cheaply.

Carnegie convinced other men to invest in a new corporation and opened his first steel mill near Pittsburgh in 1873. He expanded it and bought more mills until he was making one quarter of all the steel in America by 1900. He retired and sold his company in 1901 to J.P. Morgan, a famous banker, for 480 million dollars. Morgan formed a new corporation with it, U.S. Steel, the first billion dollar corporation in American history.

Andrew Carnegie believed it was a rich man's duty to give away his money and not die rich. After he retired from steel making, he did just that, giving away about $350 million during the rest of his life. Among his many gifts to the United States were a concert hall in New York City, a technical school in Pittsburgh, hundreds of public libraries, as well as foundations to promote education and research.

Oil. Another important industry after the Civil War was the oil industry. Oil (petroleum) was used to make fuel for heating, oils for machines, and kerosene for lighting. After the invention of the automobile, it would also be used to make gasoline. During the Gilded Age, the oil industry was totally **dominated** by one man, John D. Rockefeller, and his corporation, Standard Oil.

Rockefeller, like Carnegie, started with nothing. He began working at the age of 16 as a clerk in a produce firm in Ohio. He made some good investments and was able to get into the oil business when he was only 23. He rose very quickly to power and wealth in that business.

Rockefeller was **ruthless**. He made his products as cheaply as possible to force other manufacturers out of business. He bought out competitors and forced the railroads to give his company cheaper rates for shipping. He bribed government officials to get what he wanted. He took control of all parts of the oil industry, from taking the oil

FROM LEFT: *ANDREW CARNEGIE, CORNELIUS VANDERBILT, JOHN D. ROCKEFELLER*

out of the ground to selling it to the customer. By about 1900, Standard Oil controlled almost all oil production in the entire United States!

Inventions. New inventions helped the industries to grow and gave them new products to build and sell. The typewriter, the cash register, refrigerated railroad cars, electric trains, and the Kodak camera were all invented in the Gilded Age. The telephone and the electric light bulb were also invented during this time.

The telephone was invented by Alexander Graham Bell. Bell was a teacher for the deaf. He became interested in sending sound over wires and began learning about electricity to do it. He hired a man named Thomas Watson to help him. They built several units in the early 1870s that could send some sounds, but not all those needed to send a human voice. In 1876, he was working on his latest attempt when he spilled acid on himself. He called out, "Mr. Watson, come here. I want you!" Watson, in the other room, heard him *through the telephone* and came at once. The telephone was introduced to the world at a major industrial show in Philadelphia later that year. The Bell Telephone Company was created the next year.

The electric light bulb was one of over a thousand inventions created by America's greatest inventor, Thomas Alva Edison. Edison made an industry out of inventing. He built a laboratory, then filled it with equipment and talented assistants. He worked tirelessly to invent useful things that he could sell. He made improvements on dozens of inventions like the stock ticker, the telephone, and motion pictures. He invented the phonograph, the electric battery, a duplicating machine as well as his most famous invention, the electric light bulb.

Many people in the late 1800s were trying to find a way to make light using electricity. Edison set his lab to work on the project. He and his assistants worked for months trying to find the right filament to put inside the light bulb. He was not discouraged by his hundreds of failures. When one thing failed, he just tried something else. He said, "Genius is 1% inspiration and 99% perspiration." He believed anything could be done by hard work and he eventually did find a way to make the light bulb in 1879.

Wealth. The many new industries created many new millionaires. These newly rich people began to spend their money **lavishly**. They spent money on beautiful clothes, antiques, art from Europe, and fine horses. They built huge, ornate mansions in the cities and equally large summer "cottages" near the sea. They traveled in luxurious first class cabins on ocean ships and equally fine private railroad cars. Wealthy men built huge yachts equipped with oriental rugs, European furniture, fine china, and silver. These fancy ships were

GILDED AGE HIGH SOCIETY

scrapped without a second's hesitation if they weren't fast enough to suit the owner.

The new rich became the "high society" of America. They spent thousands of dollars on parties. They paid huge amounts to European noblemen to marry their daughters. They also gave millions to start universities, fund medical research, improve education, and promote the arts. They gave the Gilded Age its glitter with all the gold they had acquired and how fast spent it on beautiful things.

Complete these sentences.

3.13 The most famous man in the steel industry was _____ .

3.14 The man who controlled the oil industry was _____ .

3.15 _____ was a famous banker who founded U.S. Steel.

3.16 The first big corporations in America were the _____ .

3.17 _____ invented the telephone.

33

3.18 The inventor of the electric light bulb and the phonograph was_____ .

3.19 In the 1890s industry replaced _____ as America's most valuable business.

3.20 The _____ made steel making cheaper.

Answer these questions.

3.21 Who were American high society in the Gilded Age and how did they live?

_____

_____

_____

_____

3.22 How did Thomas Edison invent so many useful things?

_____

_____

_____

3.23 What did Andrew Carnegie do after he retired from the steel business?

_____

_____

_____

3.24 What happened to factories after the Civil War?

_____

_____

3.25 How did Standard Oil achieve control of the American oil industry?

_____

_____

_____

_____

Problems in Power

Immigration. The United States of America has often been called a "melting pot." That is because thousands of immigrants from all over the world have come here. They brought their ways, ideas, music, and food with them. These things were all melted together to create the America culture. That is why many Americans today drink German beer, enjoy Italian food, speak the English language, and grow Indian corn.

The huge growth of industry after the Civil War created a need for workers and that would attract many newcomers. America became the "land of opportunity" for the desperately poor of Europe. America was a land where jobs and education could mean a better life. It was a land where poor immigrants, like Carnegie, could become millionaires. From the 1870s until the 1920s millions of immigrants came from Europe to America. Every year during the last 30 years of the 19th century about 400,000 new arrivals came into the country.

Most of the immigrants before 1880 came from northern Europe: Germany, England, and Ireland. However, after that time more and more came from southern and eastern Europe: Hungary, Italy, Poland, and Russia. These people had a harder time fitting into American life. Their languages were much different. They usually could not read or write. They were not Protestant Christians, but Roman Catholic, Eastern Orthodox, or Jewish. They often did not become Americans, but stayed together to create little pieces of their homeland in the American cities. Many Americans did not like them or want them here, but they kept coming and their children as they grew up would become Americans.

These immigrants were very poor and so they stayed in the cities of the east to work in the new factories. Most were forced to live in terrible conditions in city **slums**. Large families lived in small apartments with one or two rooms. The apartments were

A FAMILY IN THE LATE 1800s IN A "SLUM" APARTMENT

Library of Congress

crawling with bugs and rats. The wood buildings caught fire easily and burned quickly. There were few toilets and the water was usually not safe. People often became ill and **epidemics** were common.

These unskilled people earned small incomes working in the steel, oil, textile, and other factories. They had no sick pay, no **pensions** for when they were old, no way to make money if they were hurt on the job, and no protection against being fired. Young children often worked also. They worked long hours in the factories tending machines, never getting to play or be outdoors. They were paid much less than adults, but their families needed every penny they could earn. Thus, the wealth of high society was taken from the hard work and suffering of the cities' poor.

Tariff. You may remember that the tariff was a big issue before the Civil War. It was a tax on goods coming into the country and it was the government's main source of money in the late 1800s. During the Civil War, the north, which wanted high tariffs, pushed them way up. After the war, the tariffs again became an important issue in industrial America.

The newly rich industry leaders loved the high tariffs. It made goods from Europe very expensive so that American-made goods could be expensive, too. They paid large bribes to Republican Congressmen who supported the tariff. They also paid large amounts of money to help tariff supporters win during elections in the late 1800s. This was part of the corruption of the time.

The tariffs were very hard on the farmers. All of the farmer's tools, clothing, and supplies cost more because of the tariff. At the same time, his crops had to be shipped on the expensive railroads and sold without any tariff to make the prices higher. Many farmers went deeply into debt to buy what they needed to run their farms. The farmers tried to push for changes, reforms. They wanted better control of the railroads, fairer taxes, and laws that would help them with their debts. However, the power of the wealthy kept the tariffs high and prevented reforms even when the American people wanted them.

Abuse of Power. During the Gilded Age, the rich industrialists had great power in America. They kept the tariffs high, treated railroad customers unfairly, and built "trusts" to control whole industries for themselves. These abuses of power led to calls for reform. However, it was not until the 1890s that reforms began to really change things. Until that time, the industrialists kept their power.

The railroads were very hard on farmers. Small farmers had no choice but to ship, using the local railroad which could charge anything. The railroads did not have one rate for everyone. Large shippers got better rates and small farmers were often charged huge amounts. Shipping goods across the country often cost less than shipping from a farm to the nearest big city. The outcry against the railroad grew so big that Congress finally did something.

In 1887, Congress passed the Interstate Commerce Act. This law required the railroads to set rates fairly and forbade the

A CARTOON SHOWING TRUSTS DESTROYING OUR COUNTRY'S LIBERTY

worst abuses. It also created the Interstate Commerce Commission to enforce the law. However, the Commission had very little power. It was a step in the right direction, but it did nothing helpful for many years.

Many of the large businesses also formed "trusts" or monopolies, businesses that controlled all sales of one product for the country. Standard Oil was the first trust, controlling oil production in America. Other trusts controlled tobacco, sugar, steel, coal, meat, and many other things people needed. Trusts could charge high prices for their goods because people could not get them anyplace else. The American people began to complain as the rich kept making more and more money by cheating the public.

Finally, Congress was pushed into acting on the trusts, too. The Sherman Anti-Trust Act was passed in 1890. It allowed the government to break apart trusts if they were harmful. Again, it was not enforced for many years, but it was the law and it would be used in the future.

Civil Service Reform. Another long-standing abuse in America was in the civil service, the people who worked for the government. You may remember that Andrew Jackson was famous for using the "spoils system," giving government jobs to his supporters. It had gotten much worse since his time. When the Republicans replaced the Democrats in power, most of the civil service was replaced, too. The same was true when the Democrats replaced the Republicans.

Also, anyone who wanted a civil service job had to pay for it. Even the woman hired to clean the offices had to give the political party in power part of her salary just to keep her job! The result was government workers who did little work and elected officials who were more interested in getting money than good workers. Thus, the public again demanded changes.

This call for reform was finally heard in 1881 when President James Garfield was assassinated by a man who was angry over not getting a job. In 1883, Congress passed a law for civil service reform. It was called the *Pendleton Act*. The Pendleton Act made it illegal for political parties to take money from government workers and gave civil service jobs to people who made the best scores on special tests. Slowly over the next 60 years, more and more jobs were filled by the people who made the best scores on the exam and not by party supporters. However, it took years to change things. As with most things from 1870 to 1890, the civil service served the rich politicians, not the poor citizens.

 Write *true* **or** *false* **in the blank.**

3.26 _____ The tariff helped farmers.

3.27 _____ America was a melting pot.

3.28 _____ Most of the immigrants after 1880 came from south and east Europe.

3.29 _____ Most of the poor immigrants took homesteads on the Great Plains.

3.30 _____ Trusts were businesses that worked for reforms.

3.31 _____ The railroads were unfair to small farmers.

3.32 _____ The Pendleton Act was for civil service reform.

3.33 _____ Immigrants saw America as a land of opportunity.

3.34 _____ Rich American industrialists did not want a high tariff.

3.35 _____ The Interstate Commerce Commission was created to enforce laws controlling the railroads.

3.36 _____ The Sherman Anti-Trust Act was written to control the railroads.

3.37 _____ During the Gilded Age, most reforms were not very successful.

3.38 _____ Children worked in the factories making the same wages as adults.

3.39 _____ Slums were dirty and unsafe places to live.

3.40 _____ Gilded Age unskilled factory workers had low pay, no sick pay and no pensions.

3.41 _____ Power during the Gilded Age was held by the rich.

3.42 _____ President Garfield was assassinated by a man who wanted trust reform.

3.43 _____ Before civil service reform, government workers often gave some of their salary to the party in power.

3.44 _____ When the political party in power changed in the 1870s, the new party usually kept the old government workers.

Before you take this last Self Test, you may want to do one or more of these self checks.

1. _____ Read the objectives. Determine if you can do them.
2. _____ Restudy the material related to any objectives that you cannot do.
3. _____ Use the SQ3R study procedure to review the material:
    a. **S**can the sections.
    b. **Q**uestion yourself again (review the questions you wrote initially).
    c **R**ead to answer your questions.
    d **R**ecite the answers to yourself.
    e **R**eview areas you didn't understand.
4. _____ Review all activities and Self Tests, writing a correct answer for each wrong answer.

SELF TEST 3

Match these people (each answer, 2 points).

3.01 _____ President assassinated by a man who did not get a civil service job

3.02 _____ President during the Civil War, freed the slaves

3.03 _____ President of the Confederacy

3.04 _____ Radical Republican leader in Reconstruction

3.05 _____ Victorious Union general, poor president

3.06 _____ Invented the telephone

3.07 _____ Standard Oil, controlled oil in America

3.08 _____ Invented the phonograph, the electric light bulb

3.09 _____ Commander of the Confederate army

3.010 _____ Steel manufacturer, spent his retirement giving away his fortune

a. Andrew Carnegie

b. John D. Rockefeller

c. Thomas Edison

d. Alexander Bell

e. James Garfield

f. Abraham Lincoln

g. Robert E. Lee

h. Ulysses S. Grant

i. Thaddeus Stevens

j. Jefferson Davis

Name the correct item, battle, person or thing (each answer, 4 points).

3.011 _____ Seward's Folly

3.012 _____ Law that gave 160 acres of land to someone for living on it five years

3.013 _____ Reason why the Great Plains were settled so quickly

3.014 _____ Civil service reform law

3.015 _____ Parts of Europe immigrants came from after 1880

3.016 _____ The time after the Civil War when the north treated the south harshly to control it and give blacks the vote

3.017 _____ The Union Pacific and the Central Pacific finished this near Ogden, Utah in 1869

3.018 _____ The Amendment that ended slavery

3.019 _____ Announcement that freed the slaves in the Confederacy

3.020 _____ American folklore heroes from the long cattle drives

Answer these questions. (each answer, 4 points).

3.021   How did the long cattle drives from Texas work?

_____

_____

_____

3.022   Who were the people of high society and how did they live?

_____

_____

_____

3.023   Why did the American industrial leaders like the tariff?

_____

_____

_____

3.024   What was a trust, like the steel trust or the sugar trust?

_____

_____

_____

3.025   How did the tariff and the railroad hurt farmers?

_____

_____

_____

Answer *true* **or** *false*. (each answer, 2 points).

3.026   _____   People settled in Alaska for the farmland.

3.027   _____   Settlers on the Great Plains often lived in sod houses.

3.028   _____   The Bessemer Process allowed companies to get oil out of the ground.

3.029   _____   After the Civil War corruption was common in government and business.

3.030   _____   The Battle of Bull Run was the turning point of the Civil War.

40

3.031 _____ Unskilled factory workers often had low wages and lived in slums.

3.032 _____ President Andrew Johnson was impeached and removed from office.

3.033 _____ Carpetbaggers were northern men who moved south to make money and work for the government after the Civil War.

3.034 _____ Most reforms did not succeed in the Gilded Age.

3.035 _____ Immigrants came to America because it was the land of opportunity.

$\dfrac{80}{100}$

Score
Teacher Check _____
_____
Initial   **Date**

Before you take the LIFEPAC Test, you may want to do one or more of these self checks.

1. _____ Read the objectives. Determine if you can do them.
2. _____ Restudy the material related to any objectives that you cannot do.
3. _____ Use the SQ3R study procedure to review the material.
4. _____ Review all activities and Self Tests, and LIFEPAC Glossary.
5. _____ Restudy areas of weakness indicated by the last Self Test.